POLITICAL SCIENCE FOR KIDS

Democracy, Communism & Socialism

Politics for Kids

6th Grade Social Studies

BABY PROFESSOR

EDUCATION KIDS

Speedy Publishing LLC
40 E. Main St. #1156
Newark, DE 19711
www.speedypublishing.com
Copyright 2018

I n this book, we're going to talk about democracy, communism, and socialism. So, let's get right to it!

Democracy

Dictatorship

Aristocracy

Monarchy

Democracy, communism, and socialism are all different types of government structures. In almost all cases, the governments of different countries operate using modified forms of these government models.

Republic

Anarchy

WHAT IS A DEMOCRACY?

In a democracy, government officials are elected by the citizens of the country. In other words, citizens living in a democratic country have the opportunity to cast their votes for the people they want in positions of governmental power as well as for the laws they want passed.

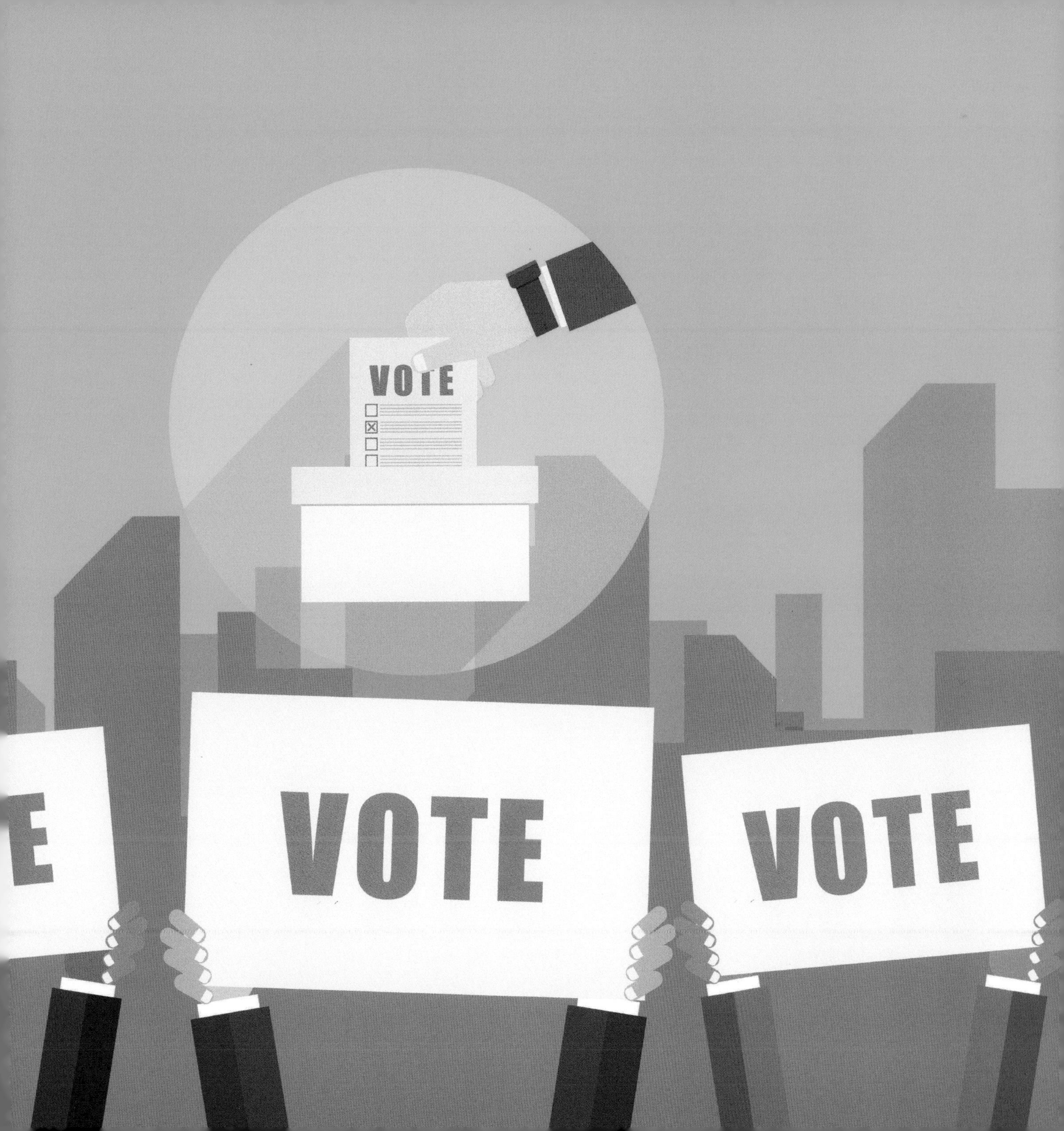
VOTE
E
VOTE
VOTE

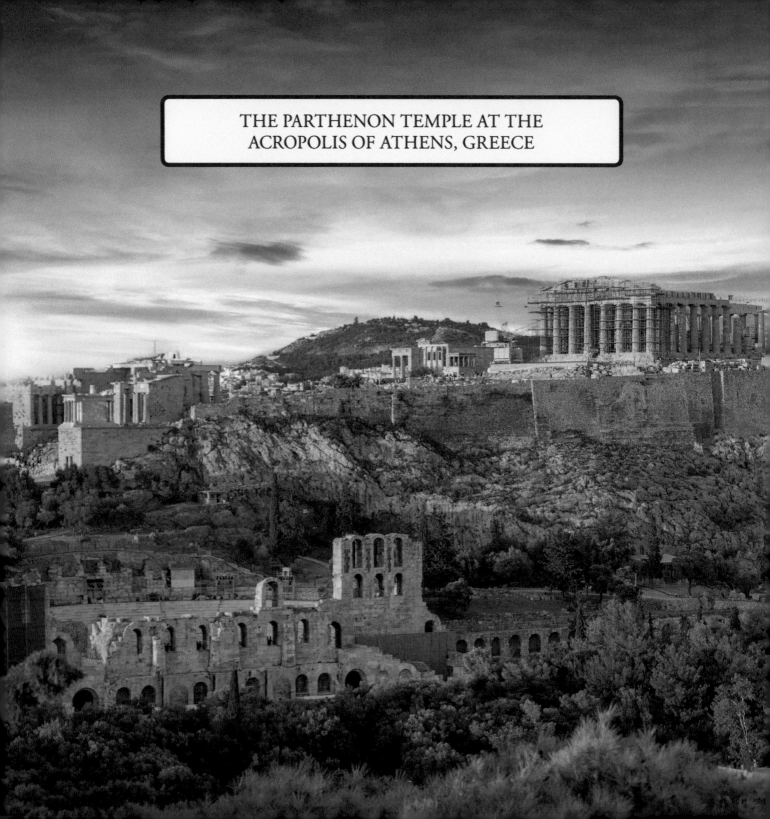

THE PARTHENON TEMPLE AT THE
ACROPOLIS OF ATHENS, GREECE

TYPES OF DEMOCRACY

Democracy can be direct or it can be representative.

Direct Democracy

Athens, the city-state of ancient Greece, operated under a direct democracy. In fact, "democracy" comes from the Greek language. The word "demos" in Greek translates to "people." The Athenian citizens would come to the central plaza to cast their votes. Every citizen would be allowed to cast a vote for every crucial decision in the government. Of course, at that time, only men were allowed to vote.

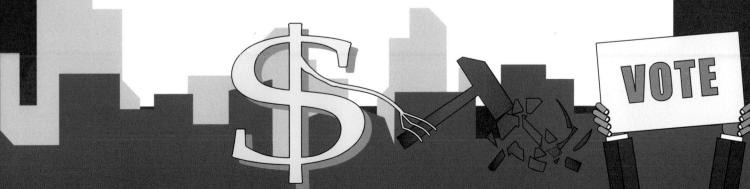

Representative Democracy

There are over 320 million people living in the United States. As the population of a city or country increases, it's not practical for everyone to have a direct vote.

The next best method is to elect representatives who will handle the decisions on direct issues. This is the way the United States government operates.

PRESIDENTIAL CANDIDATES

The people vote for the president and the members of Congress. Once elected, these representatives run the country and make the day-to-day decisions. The United States can be described as either a representative democracy or a democratic republic.

TOP CHARACTERISTICS OF DEMOCRATIC GOVERNMENTS

Not all democracies operate in exactly the same way, but most democracies have some characteristics in common.

The citizens cast direct votes or cast votes indirectly through their elected representatives.

GROUP OF AMERICAN POLITICIANS
STANDING ON THE STAGE

A PERSON CASTING A BALLOT AT A
POLLING STATION DURING ELECTION

The elections are open and fair. All the citizens in the country have voting privileges. Citizens of every race, religion, income status, and gender are encouraged to vote. Citizens need to actively participate in their government for it to work optimally.

Even though the majority vote will decide which candidates are elected and which laws are passed, there are certain rights that each individual has, such as the right to practice his or her choice of religion.

THE WHITE HOUSE IN WASHINGTON D.C.
ON A CLOUDY DAY, EXECUTIVE OFFICE OF
THE PRESIDENT OF THE UNITED STATES

The lawmakers and officials in the government have power, but their power isn't unlimited. There are checks and balances to ensure that they stay within their limits. Also, they are only allowed to stay in their positions for a limited period of time.

DISADVANTAGES OF DEMOCRACIES

No form of government is perfect and even democracy has its disadvantages.

Some of the disadvantages are:

- It costs a great deal of money to run for public office so only people who are quite wealthy with wealthy connections can afford to run for office, especially for the higher-level positions.
- Voters are sometimes not well educated about the issues for which they are casting their votes.

DISHONEST POLITICIAN

- If there are only two main political parties, such as the Republicans and Democrats in the United States, there are only limited choices for candidates and issues.
- Sometimes the government is slow-moving and decisions take a long time to make.
- Despite these issues, democracy is a very successful form of government and people who live in democratic countries tend to have a high standard of living. In fact, some of the world's richest countries are democracies.

HOW IS DEMOCRACY CONNECTED WITH CAPITALISM?

Democracy is a form of government that allows for a lot of freedom. The economy in a democracy allows for private ownership of real estate and businesses. This type of economy is called capitalism and is frequently described as a "free market" system. Capitalism exists under other forms of government as well. There are three very important tenets of capitalism:

Capitalism

Private Ownership

In a capitalistic economy, individuals own businesses, real estate and factories. The government may have some regulations in place, but private citizens make most of the decisions about how their businesses should be run.

Free Competition

Free competition ensures that the quality of products will remain high and prices will be kept in check. Consumers should get the best products for the prices they pay because there is lots of competition and lots of choices.

A WOMAN IS OVERWHELMED WITH THE WIDE RANGE OF PRODUCTS IN THE SUPERMARKET WHEN SHOPPING.

Supply and Demand

The government doesn't set the prices for products. Instead, prices are determined by the constant ebb and flow of supply and demand.

WHAT IS COMMUNISM?

In 1848, two German philosophers, Karl Marx and his colleague Friedrich Engels, published a pamphlet called the Communist Manifesto. They pointed out that capitalistic societies were creating a very uneven wealth distribution. There was a huge gap between the poor and the rich. Many people were working very hard, but only a few people were reaping the benefits of the wealth that they were creating.

STATUE OF KARL MARX AND
FRIEDRICH ENGELS

The authors of the Communist Manifesto felt that there would soon be uprisings across the world to combat the injustice caused by capitalism. They felt that workers around the world were being treated unfairly by their bosses and that these oppressed workers would rise up against the capitalist management.

TOP CHARACTERISTICS OF COMMUNIST GOVERNMENTS

In the Communist Manifesto, Marx and Engel described the basic tenets of a Communist government.

Individuals wouldn't own property. The government would own all property.

There would be just one government bank.

Income would be taxed and those who earned more would be taxed more.

The government would control how the workers would work and how they would be paid.

No one would inherit property or have individual property rights.

SCHOOL IN NORTH KOREA KNOWN
TO BE A COMMUNIST COUNTRY

The government would control all the financial aspects of education as well as transportation and communication. Farms and factories would be run by the government.

The idea was that everyone should have an equal amount of wealth and that the wealth generated among the workers should be shared equally by the workers, but in practice this didn't occur.

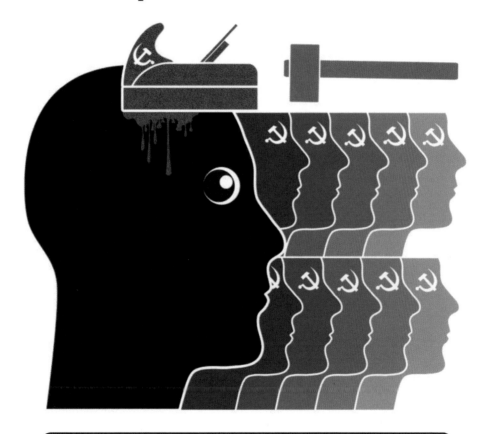

COMMUNISM AND EQUALITY.
PEOPLE IN COMMUNISTIC POLITICAL
SYSTEMS TURN INTO SLAVES

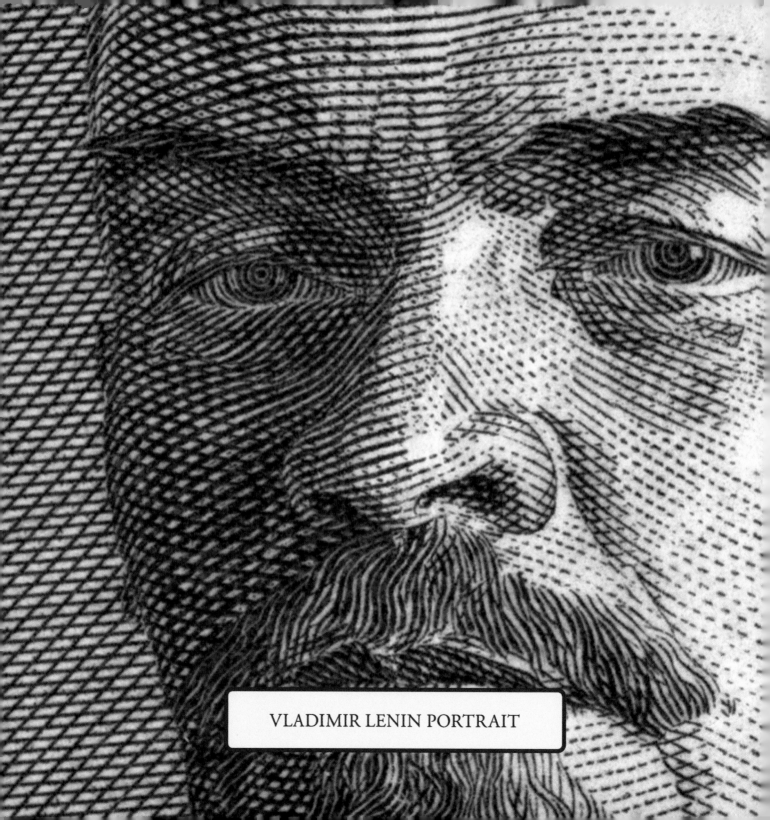

VLADIMIR LENIN PORTRAIT

COMMUNISM IN RUSSIA

Vladimir Lenin was influenced by Marx's theories. He started a political party called the Bolshevik party. They overthrew the government of Russia in October of 1917. They renamed the country the "Soviet Union." During World War II, the Soviets joined the countries of the United States, the United Kingdom, and China to fight against Nazi Germany and Hitler.

However, soon after the war was over, the Soviets began to take control of many of the countries in Eastern Europe. They became a superpower like the United States and the threat of communism was a constant source of tension that was called the "Cold War."

COMMUNISM IN CHINA

The Chinese Civil War took place from 1927 until 1950. The Communists won the war and took over the Chinese government. Mao Zedong became the Chairman of the Communist Party in China and the ruler of the government.

THE END RESULTS OF COMMUNISM

People living under Communist rule have very few freedoms compared to those living in Democratic countries. Sometimes they are not allowed to practice religion. They are not allowed to own property. Officials in the government often become very powerful and they abuse their power.

BUDDHISM

CATHOLICISM

ISLAM

ORTHODOXY

HINDUISM

JUDAISM

IN COMMUNISM IT IS NOT ALLOWED
TO PRACTICE RELIGION

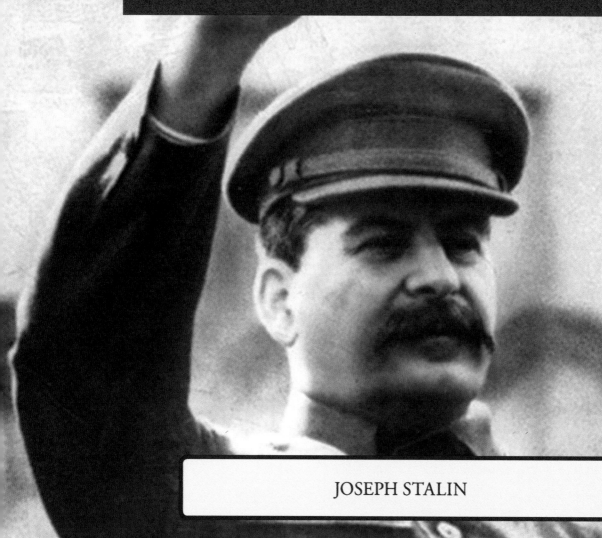

Evil leaders, such as Joseph Stalin in the Soviet Union, have been responsible for killing millions of workers instead of protecting them and ensuring that they shared the wealth as Marxism had proposed.

JOSEPH STALIN

When Mao Zedong was the ruler of China, the level of poverty was over 50%.

Today, China has instituted many reforms to ensure that their citizens have a higher standard of living. China, North Korea, Vietnam, Laos, and Cuba are the only major countries that currently have communist governments.

NIGHT SKYLINE IN SHANGHAI, CHINA

THE SICKLE AND HAMMER ARE
A SIGN OF SOCIALISM.

WHAT IS SOCIALISM?

The main goal of socialism, in theory, is to make the gap between the wealthy and the poor smaller. Socialists believe that the government should distribute wealth in a way that makes it fair for everyone. They feel that production and manufacturing should be organized and managed by the people, either in a direct way or through the guidance and management of the government.

These theories are similar to Communism, however Socialists don't think that workers should rise up and use violence to change the capitalistic system. They also don't want to get rid of private property completely.

Social Security Disability Claim

General Questions

Proposed Insured's Name:
(Please use capital letters)

Gender: ○ Male ○ Female   Passport no:

Email Address:

Social Security Number:

Birth Date:

Address: Others   Are you a retiree? ○ Yes ○ No

Phone Number:

ID Number: ○ Single ○ Married ○ Devorced

Status:

Occupation: Children: ○ Yes ○ No
Plan Choice:

Personal Details

Name of Beneficiary :

Bank Account : (or ID number for confirmation only)   Spouse: ○ Yes ○ No
Plan Choice:

Name and Address of beneficiary's bank :

Employee: ○ Yes ○ No
Plan Choice: ...per week**
...tion fees apply)
...17

● PLAN B JOIN NOW !
Starting from THB $21 per week**
(prices excl. VAT.)
See more details on page 17

...nual Premium:
...Monthly PAT (co...

Even the United States, which is a democratic, capitalistic country, has many social programs, such as Social Security, to protect the disabled, the weak, and the elderly.

SUMMARY

Democracy is a form of government. Democratic governments allow their citizens many individual freedoms. Citizens in democratic countries are allowed to participate in free elections so they can choose the representatives they want to make decisions and run the government. Capitalism is a "free market" system practiced in democratic countries. Communism doesn't allow for a "free market."

KARL MARX

Originally, the Communism that Karl Marx described was created to equalize wealth across society so there wouldn't be a huge gap between the rich property owners and the poor workers.

Unfortunately, Communism didn't protect the workers. Instead, workers were abused by the government. Socialism is similar to Communism in some respects. However, Socialists don't believe that private property should be completely eliminated or that violence should be used to rise up against capitalism.

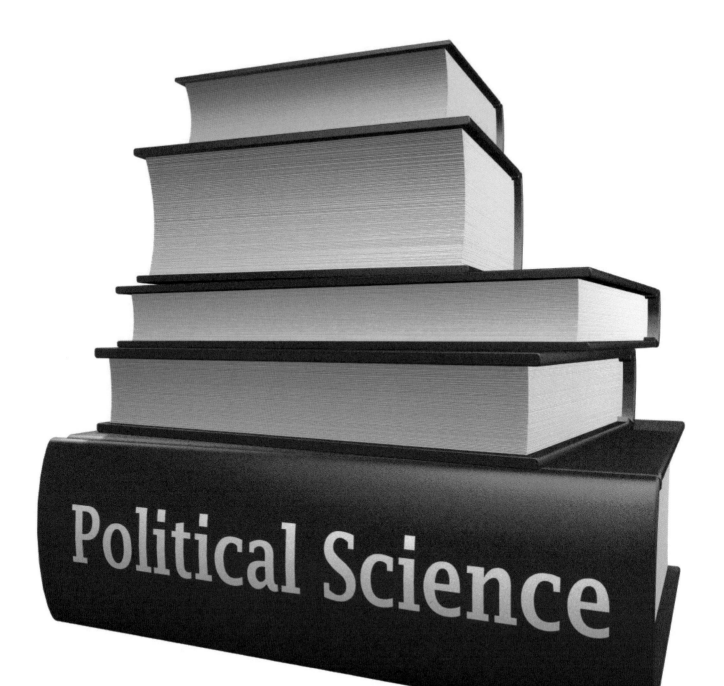
Political Science

Now that you've read about democracy, communism, and socialism, you may want to read about the Magna Carta and democracy in the Baby Professor book:

King John, The Magna Carta and Democracy - History for Kids Books | Children's European History.

Visit

BABY PROFESSOR
EDUCATION KIDS

www.BabyProfessorBooks.com

to download Free Baby Professor eBooks
and view our catalog of new and exciting
Children's Books

36546496R00037

Printed in Great Britain
by Amazon